Psychological Triggers

How to Use the Dark Secret Techniques of Psychology to Control, Influence, Persuade and Manipulate Anyone

By Dan Crosby

I0455309

Table of Contents

Book Description.. 4

Introduction 7

Chapter 1: Psychological Triggers......................10

Chapter 2: The Basic Principle behind All
Behaviors... 23

Chapter 3: Needs: The Game Changer 32

Chapter 4: Logic 40

Chapter 5: Feeling Of Significance 47

Chapter 6: Anticipation 54

Chapter 7: Relating To Others 61

Chapter 8: Authenticity 67

Chapter 9: Curiosity 73

Chapter 10: Social Proof 81

Chapter 11: Scarcity.. 90

Conclusion... 97

Book Description

Do you struggle to get people to listen to you, to have them comply with instructions and requests? Have you ever wanted to become a great persuader? Do you ever think about how great it would be to control and manipulate **anyone** you wanted?

Well, what if I told you that there are various ways to do so, and that you can easily use them throughout your business and personal life to great effect, enabling you to get what you want with children, adults, spouses, friends, colleagues, bosses, subordinates, students, teachers, and practically anyone you encounter in your daily life!

"Psychological Triggers: How to Use the Dark Secret Techniques of Psychology to Control, Influence, Persuade and Manipulate Anyone" contains invaluable insights into how to achieve unbeatable success in an ever more competitive world.

Who Can Benefit From This Book?

Let's be honest: It is chaos out there. Millions of people are striving to get noticed, struggling to stand in the light, to be different. If you are one of these people, determined to be someone, whom not only wants to be noticed but absolutely **must** stand out and get to the top, then this book is for you. Think of it as your guide to the heights.

Getting your way with people and knowing how to persuade, influence, control and manipulate them will help you achieve incredible levels of success in whatever field you operate in.

Teachers, students, parents, children, husbands, wives, boyfriends, girlfriends, bachelors, businessmen, supervisors, colleagues or subordinates, in short *anyone* with the right mindset can reap the benefits delivered by this book. It doesn't matter what group you belong to: If you want to do better in life, this book is for you!

How Can This Book Help You?

If used correctly this book can help you achieve the success that you have been yearning for since as far back as you can remember; since that first realization that you were special: That you deserve the very best in life.

Read each unit thoroughly, take care to pay attention to every word and reinforce the concepts by rereading the last part of every chapter, the "How to Use This to Influence and Manipulate People" sections. Take notes. Study and put it to memory. Here actual techniques are provided with real examples that will help you learn and understand the power of psychological triggers that you will use in your pursuit of success.

Introduction

New to college and full of excitement I was delighted to have gotten into such a prestigious institution. All my hard work during high school had finally paid off. I was going to kill it at college. I was going to do great, I was absolutely convinced of it.

Except I didn't and I was totally wrong.

Within a very short time I realized that college was like nothing I had experienced before. The rules were different, in fact everything that people did, and the way in which they behaved, was nothing like high school.

Teachers had loved me in high school, I was popular and I had had many friends. Here, everyone seemed to be hostile. Everyone wanted to be on top. The professors seemed to be aggressive creatures, intent on doing anything and everything to make you feel like an absolute nobody. It didn't take long for me to lose confidence in myself. The rock star student faded into the background and an under-confident, insignificant "yes-man" took his place, a person who had no idea how to stand out.

That is when hiding out in the college library that I came across Robert Cialdini's, "Influence: The Psychology of Persuasion". Now, I don't want it to sound like a cliché, but it truly changed my life. I suddenly knew that success could be achieved in one simple way: By learning the art of persuasion and influence, because the moment you know how to get your way with people, the rest comes easily.

This book is undoubtedly inspired by the work of Mr. Cialdini and his book, Influence: The Psychology of Persuasion.

Psychological Triggers are tools that can be used to put the people that you want to persuade or influence into a certain state of mind, a state in which they are much more likely to be persuaded.

The following eleven chapters discuss different psychological triggers that can be used to get what you want, every single time. I thoroughly explain and demonstrate the way in which each trigger works, how it effects everyday decisions and, specifically, how it can be used to manipulate, control, and influence people.

If you want to make the most out of the book please do take notes, and thoroughly study the techniques that you would like to use. Moreover, practice all of the techniques that you think might be beneficial to **you**. Practice every day. Make yourself a promise to do so. Without practice this book will just be another paperweight but with self-training, it can become your very own ladder to success.

Happy reading!

Chapter 1: Psychological Triggers

I can recall this day from my high school pretty clearly. I had finally gone ahead and registered myself for the talent show. Every one kept on telling me what a beautiful voice I had, and that I should sing for the crowd so that my talent could be recognized. I was all for it, but my problem was an intense nervousness that overpowered me every time I thought of performing in front of a crowd. Nevertheless, this time I had taken the plunge.

On Sunday, I dressed up for the performance. Mom had made an early dinner of mac and cheese. I ate some of it and left for school. Finally, it was time. They called my name and I felt sick to my stomach. I tried to step onto the stage with shaking legs but oh wait... I felt really sick. The next moment I was vomiting all over the stage carpet. Oh, the embarrassment of throwing up in front of a huge crowd. I am sure you can understand.

It's been nearly twenty years since that event, and although I have gotten over my stage fright, there is still one thing I still cannot stand, the sight and smell of; perhaps you can guess what it is? You guessed right! Its mac and cheese.

What Are Psychological Triggers?

After reading this horrifying story, you must be wondering why on earth I would divulge the details of such an intensely private high school tragedy. Well, it is because later, this story helped me understand the concept of psychological triggers in a very significant way.

Why can't I stand the sight or smell of mac and cheese? It is because mac and cheese bring back those feelings of intense humiliation, of the shame that I felt in front of the whole school. I feel disgusted, agitated, and even angry with myself.

When seeing, hearing, touching, smelling, or tasting something "triggers" certain feelings or thoughts within you, that something becomes your very own "psychological trigger". Sound complicated? Well, please don't worry, because it isn't.

Hardees is notorious for their suggestive and innuendo filled advertising campaign in many countries. Why would they go ahead and base their marketing on sexual innuendo? It is because they know that these suggestions evoke feelings of pleasure in a large number of potential customers, and happy people make good business. It is as simple as that!

In the *Hardees* campaign what they portray triggers feelings of sexual attraction in potential customers, which then turns them into **actual** customers.

To conclude, psychological triggers are tools that can bring about certain feelings (Happiness, fear, guilt, etc.) in people, making them more prone to influence, persuasion, and manipulation.

You can have your very own, personalized triggers, and then there are some triggers that are common to a very large number of people. Most advertisements make use of triggers that are applicable to at least one specific target market.

Psychological triggers don't only have wide and impressive implications for sales and marketing, they have the potential to unlock a much more impressive you. You too can learn how to use psychological triggers to be more influential and persuasive, to have people do whatt you want. Just like companies get their marketing team to buy their products. It's the exact same application of the same theory; in fact there isn't an aspect of life in which you cannot benefit from understanding, and mastering, psychological triggers.

Why It Is Important To Know About Them?

My daughter loves to go out for ice cream on Saturday nights. Last Saturday morning, I promised her that I would take her out if she first finished her homework. She did finish her homework, but then I remembered that I had made an appointment with my dentist for that very evening, something I had forgotten about. "But you promised that you would take me out if I finished my homework!" Sally said, and I had no choice but to call to reschedule my appointment.

Sally made use of a fundamental principle in the psychology of persuasion and influence, without even realizing it. We have to act consistently with our previous statements and actions, for no other reason than that is how we are designed.

In similar ways, psychological triggers have applications throughout life. Be it in parenting or leadership, teaching or management, psychological triggers can help you be a better persuader. The use of psychological triggers can help you get people to do what you want, without them even realizing it.

The art of influence will help you in all areas of your life. At home, you can be a better parent or spouse, by learning the use of psychological triggers. At the workplace, you can be a better boss, subordinate, or colleague.

If you are in a profession that can make use of the art of persuasion, manipulation and influence, then psychological triggers can be your best friend. You must be wondering now, how --and why-- do psychological triggers work?

Triggers make use of the **peripheral route of mental processing**, as opposed to the **central route of mental processing**. Sound like a lot of jargon that you would rather not listen to? Well, please let me explain because this is a really important step in our journey to mastering these techniques.

Human beings can process information that is provided to them via one of two routes i.e. the central and the peripheral route. The central route requires deeper processing; hence we might make use of the central route while making the decision to buy a very expensive piece of technology, or machinery. We think through the details of its features, components and specifications, so that we can make an informed decision after extensive deliberation and consideration.

Conversely, when we use peripheral route processing, we make the decision to buy on the basis of a certain **emotional appeal**, or a singular feature of the item that we find attractive. Simply put, we are not interested in extensive deliberation when peripheral route processing is used. For example, we are more likely to use peripheral route processing while buying a quart of orange juice than when, say, buying a Canon camera.

Advertisements mostly make use of peripheral route processing. Why? Well, human beings have finite mental resources at any given time. Even Einstein would not have had enough mental capacity to give extensive deliberation to an impulse purchase, because that's the way we are wired, especially if we don't have a lot to lose if the decision turns out to be a bad one. If we pay $15 for sneakers that fall apart after a month, it's not really a problem. It's **only** $15.

Psychological triggers mostly use this peripheral route of processing. Now you know why it is essential to know about it. We base most of our decisions on the simple cues that we are constantly bombarded with; we scarcely give these 'light' decisions any thought.

Psychological triggers can thus come in very handy in situations where people do not have the time, motivation or the mental resources to actually **think about a decision**.

Here is an example: Have you ever bought something expensive in the belief that if it is expensive it must be of top-notch quality? I know I have, and I would be lying if I said that I haven't made decisions on the basis of the assumption: expensive = good. I am probably prone to making decisions on the basis of this assumption even after having extensively studied and implemented psychological triggers.

Triggers have a way of sneaking in, even when you think you have out-smarted them. Like I just mentioned, knowing about triggers doesn't necessarily mean that you won't fall prey to their dastardly trickery!

One example of this is the pricing technique. Have you ever wondered why prices on tags read $9.99 instead of simply $10? You guessed right. It's a kind of psychological trigger that makes you think that $9.99 is closer to $9. The reality, of course, is very different.

I will now dive in to reveal the details of several more psychological triggers. For now, it is important to note that once you have mastered the use of psychological triggers, your power to influence and persuade will increase exponentially. Psychological triggers have the power to bring us success, **if** we figure out how to use them with maximum effect.

Understanding Psychological Triggers Can Make Life Easier For You

So now we know that there are hardly any areas in life where psychological triggers don't have some kind of application.

Relationships: Do you like someone and have no idea how to make them return your feelings? You are not alone. Millions of people face this problem and let me tell you, if you learn to use psychological triggers correctly, conveying your feelings and having them reciprocated will become so easy that you'll wonder as to why it seemed so impossible before.

Business and Work: Psychological triggers can make closing business deals a piece of cake. If you have trouble making the other party see why closing a deal would be beneficial for them, the use of psychological triggers can help you overcome this seemingly insurmountable wall. Similarly, if you are having problems with a subordinate in getting him to do what you want, the use of psychological triggers can achieve that aim for you. Moreover, if you are having trouble getting a point across to your boss, there are several psychological triggers that you can use to help in that situation as well.

Altruism: So far psychological triggers might sound like something dark and evil, something that you can use to manipulate people in a bad way. It doesn't have to be that way, of course. You can use psychological triggers to genuinely help people understand what is better for them. It truly can be something exceptionally beneficial for all involved.

Parenting: If you are struggling with defiant teenagers who just won't listen to you, their teachers or peers then don't worry, because, as is often the case with issues such as these, you are not the only one facing the serious problems teenagers can bring into the home. Psychological triggers will help you communicate with them effectively. Once communication is established problems are reduced and quickly start to move towards becoming solutions.

Teaching: Psychological triggers have many applications in teaching. Getting your point across to students is easier when psychological triggers are used intelligently.

Chapter Summary: The Key Points

- Psychological triggers are tools that can be used to give rise to particular feelings in individuals, which can then make them act or think in predictable ways. Psychological triggers are the perfect tools for arming yourself with techniques to influence, persuade and manipulate.

- Psychological triggers are important because human beings have **limited mental capacity** and more often than not they are only using a minimum of their mental faculties for any one decision at any one time. Psychological triggers go via the peripheral route of processing (the one that makes use of automatic decision making and thus utilizes minimum mental resources). They can therefore be used to **effectively** influence and persuade in numerous life situations.

- Psychological triggers can be used in teaching, parenting and personal and business relationships to gain influence and persuade people to do as **you** want.

Chapter 2: The Basic Principle behind All Behaviors

Dave, 52 years of age, had spent most of his life in a sluggish manner, happy to be a couch potato at every given chance, he wouldn't even go out for a walk. When he was 50 years old he was diagnosed with coronary heart disease and ended up having a bypass. That is what changed his life. Now, at 52 years old, he decided to run a marathon. All his friends thought he was crazy, but he was set on it.

*While running the marathon he sprained his ankle and ended up with a really bad knee injury, **but** he finished it and was finally happy despite all the physical injuries that he had sustained.*

"He was happy despite suffering physical injuries", what does this tell us? This lets us in on an open secret. **All human behavior is driven by a need to avoid pain and gain pleasure.** Dave did something painful because he associated pleasure with the end result i.e. completing the marathon.

What Drives Our Behavior?

Human beings are simple, they want to be happy. Hence the best way to influence and persuade people is to first make them happy. See? The art of persuasion is not some kind of rocket science, you just have to do things that make people happy and **ta**-*daa*, you have them doing what you want.

This is basically what Dale Carnegie tells us in his bestseller, "How to Make Friends and Influence People." Stop criticizing people, start to appreciate and encourage, be emphatic, keep smiling, and be genuinely interested. All these things basically make people happy and thus more prone to listening and acting upon what we have to say.

Why do you think fire fighters risk their lives to jump into raging infernos and save lives? They are not insane, they just associate pleasure with helping people, or maybe because they like to take risks. Either way, what guides their behavior is the desire to attain pleasure.

Each and every psychological trigger mentioned in this book is based upon this one basic principle. We are motivated to complete many of our daily activities due to this core idea.

How Does This Effect Every Day Decisions?

I cannot begin to emphasize the importance of this principle in our daily decision-making. You wake up and decide to make a luxurious breakfast, perhaps a big plate of bacon and eggs. Why? Because eating comfort food will make you happy!

You decide to go on a blind date, even though you do not really like the idea of spending time with a total stranger, who **may** or *may not* be your type. But in the end, going on this one blind date might help you find your soul mate. So, we're even prepared to do something that we don't really like because the end result holds the promise of making us happy.

You see, each and every one of our decisions is based upon this principle. There is hardly any exception to this rule. Even if we do something for other people, out of the pure goodness of heart, in the end it will bring YOU happiness. It is just like how Joey out of NBC's 90s comedy Friends says: *"There is no selfless good deed."*

How to Use This to Influence and Manipulate People

Now that you know that all human behavior, and pretty much each and every one of our everyday decisions, is based upon the desire to avoid pain and gain pleasure, you can use this principle to influence, persuade, manipulate and control people. How? Let's see:

In sales, you have to know what your customers associate with pleasure and pain. Some people might associate pleasure with fighting fires;

others might hate the idea of it. Let's start with something that almost everyone loves: Family!

Can you recall any TV advertisements that employ the concept of family life?

There are numerous TV ads that use happy families in order to boost their sales. So there you have it: the feelings of pleasure are used to boost sales. Every time you see a happy family eating from a jar of *Nutella*, you are going to associate those feelings of marital or family bliss with that image and end up buying a huge jar of *Nutella*.

The pleasure principle doesn't just work in TV advertisements, it can work in everyday situations as well. For example, how are you going to get your temperamental teenager to attend the family meal? You definitely have to bait them with something that they like and associate with pleasure. Do they have someone special they like? Every teenager usually does. You can bait them by saying that their cousin is probably going to bring some of the cute /

handsome friends that they like to the family gathering... *wink, wink.*

Make sure you bait them with something that is actually going to be true though. Empty promises are just going to affect your power to persuade in the future.

Similarly, you can utilize this pleasure psychological trigger during a job interview. Let's imagine that the interviewer is a supervisor who wants to wind a project up once and for all. They want to get from point A (where the project is right now) to point Z (where the project will be at completion). You can persuade the interviewer to hire you by making them think that you have it all figured out until, let's say, point Y, so to get to point Z, all they have to do is hire you!

You can do this by saying, *"I have a very specific plan in mind to increase productivity. Your employees will stay motivated throughout the day and will be fully utilizing their on the job time. It will only take me a month to implement that plan after you hire me."*

See how cleverly the interviewee took the interviewer to point Y, and if they want to get to point Z, they will have to hire them! The interviewer is far more likely to hire them after the interviewee has given the prospective employer a little taste of the success that the firm will experience after the hire.

Can you think of some other scenarios in which the pleasure-pain psychological trigger can be implemented?

The tendency to avoid pain works in the same way, it actually works *even more* than the motivation to gain pleasure. This phenomenon is known as **negativity bias** i.e. humans make more effort to avoid pain than to gain pleasure.

Have a look at the following client testimonial:

"We searched for an uncomplicated and strong time-tracking tool with an easy-to-use interface for a long time. We are very happy with *Harvest*, which provided simple implementation and meaningful output of information."

This testimonial was on the website of a time tracking tool. See how they have made use of the pain-avoiding principle. The message conveyed is that by using this product, and not one of their competitors' tracking-tools, employees will be able to avoid several complications that are nothing more than an avoidable hassle.

How can you make use of the pain-avoidance principle in other life situations?

You can use this principle in teaching. When a teacher says to her students, *"Now, you don't want to write your homework assignment five times, do you? So complete your home work on time."*

The teacher just made use of the fundamental pain-avoidance principle to successfully have her students complete their assignment on time. In the same way, these pleasure seeking and pain avoidance psychological triggers can be used across a number of life situations. You can use it to manipulate, control and influence people... once you get the hang of using it properly.

Chapter Summary: The Key Points

- The basic principle behind all human behavior is the tendency to avoid pain and gain pleasure.
- This principle can be used in sales, marketing and several other life situations to influence, manipulate, control and persuade people.

Chapter 3: Needs: The Game Changer

Maslow's hierarchy is a well-known concept. Even if you haven't heard of it before, you must be aware that human behavior is largely guided by needs. Why did you get up in the middle of the night? Because you felt the need to pee. Why did you apply for the position of Class President? Because you felt the need to shine and stand out. Why did you help that homeless man on the street? Because you felt the need to find meaning in your life by helping others.

Needs and Their Importance

Your basic human needs are of deep significance in the field of persuasion and influence. Maslow's hierarchy assumes that all human behavior takes place according to a set hierarchical of needs. The needs outlined below take the shape of a pyramid, with the first being at the base.

First are biological needs; the needs of hunger, thirst, and sleep etc. Biological needs outweigh all other human needs. These are the basic needs that generally require fulfillment before all others.

Second in the hierarchy are safety needs. These include the needs for a safe home, a stable life, and a lawful society etc.

Third in the hierarchy are love and a feeling of belonging. Human beings have a need to love and be loved, to relate, and to be social. These needs come in at the middle of the hierarchy.

Fourth in the hierarchy are esteem needs. We need to achieve, we need to have a reputation, and we need to have a social status etc.

Lastly, at the top of the pyramid, lie the self-actualization needs. Maslow believed that all human beings have a need for self-fulfillment and growth. Although not everyone reaches the top of the pyramid, this is the highest level of need that a person can have.

Good advertisements make use of one or many of these essential aspects of the human psyche. We witness the application of these needs everywhere in our daily lives. For example, the employer who offers great working conditions with fantastic fringe benefits to their employees are actually fulfilling the fundamental human needs of their workers. The workers will then be much more easily persuaded to work hard, honestly, and with a real sense of worth.

Maslow's hierarchy of needs has plenty of application in sales as well. Human beings work on these basic motivation principles, so learning how to utilize them in advertising and marketing can prove to be very beneficial for profits. Sales can be increased exponentially by focusing marketing strategies on the very basic needs that a particular product can fulfill.

How Needs Effect Every Day Decisions?

Our everyday decisions are largely based upon our basic needs. Therefore, to persuade effectively, we have to make people see that by listening to what we are saying, many of their needs will be fulfilled.

For example, one everyday decision that we all have is choosing the brand of coffee that you are going to have in your kitchen. Coffee advertisements can focus on several human needs for maximum sales. They can, for instance, show a group of friends having a cup of coffee together at home having a great time. This will make you feel that after buying this brand of coffee, your social needs will be fulfilled.

How To Use Needs To Influence And Manipulate People?

When people's base needs are threatened, their focus cannot move to any of their higher needs. This is a dark technique that has been used by many manipulators in history. When the poor masses are focused on their biological and safety needs, none of them can actually rise above these immediate threats and so they miss the danger posed by a potential dictator.

There are instances in history by which poison was used to incapacitate kings and queens without actually murdering them. They became so engrossed in protecting and realizing their safety needs that they ended up having no focus left for esteem and self-actualization. They failed to express the main purpose to be: the act of ruling.

You can use needs to persuade people in other ways. Try to figure out what needs a particular person is presently focused on. Try to cater to those needs and you will be thanked. For example, you can persuade people to give money to a specific cause by telling them that several other residents of the housing development that they are living in have also agreed to donate to the same cause. In this way, you will be targeting their need for community and relatedness and it is very likely that they will agree to donate to your cause too.

You can also bring people's attention to their higher-order needs, the ones they are most likely not paying attention to at the moment. You will have reached incredible heights of persuasion once you get people to see that there are greater things in life than fulfilling social, safety, and physiological needs.

Here are some other ways in which you can use needs as psychological triggers to influence and persuade:

1. Remind people of a need. For example, say: *"If you take this toy home, it is going to make your child's day."* See how in this effective approach the persuader has succeeded in reminding the potential customer of his love needs. Jot down five such sentences right now and practice

them today. Remember them and store them away, ready to be used at the next opportunity.

2. Threaten people's lower-order needs: For example: "Are you sure that you will be able to survive without this five-figure income?" Note how the safety need is threatened in order to get a person to comply. Write five such need-threatening sentences yourself and practice them. Again, put them to memory and have them on hand ready to be used at the next opportunity.

3. Recognize people's current needs: For example, "I know that you want to show your employees who is boss. Read this handout and you will be thanking me later." Note how the persuader recognizes the supervisor's esteem needs and markets his product by using their current needs. Write five such sentences yourself: practice, remember, and use them.

Chapter Summary: The Key Points

- The Five Levels of Human Needs are **biological**, **safety**, **love**, **esteem**, and **self-actualization**. Lower order needs have to be fulfilled in order to reach higher order needs.

- You can use these to persuade and manipulate people in many ways. You can bring their focus on the things that your product, or whatever you have to offer, will provide to their lives.

- You can also influence people by reminding them of their present needs and by threatening others.

Chapter 4: Logic

Over two thousand years ago, Aristotle passed away. You must be laughing at this obvious statement of fact. Everyone knows that Aristotle died. What you might not know that before he did, he left us a legacy of knowledge on persuasion and influence.

Ethos, Pathos and Logos were three modes of persuasion given by Aristotle. Ethos refers to the credibility of the speaker, Pathos refers to the emotional appeal in speech and Logos refers to the logics, or logical appeal in an argument.

To influence and persuade, you need to get the hang of all three of these rhetorical appeals and more importantly, you need to learn to apply all of them effectively. In the previous chapters, we focused mainly on psychological triggers that took the peripheral route of processing i.e. they appeal to the emotional side of our fundamental needs.

Logic is different; it takes the central route of processing. So those people who actually listen and focus are more likely to be persuaded by logical appeal more than anything else. Moreover, there are situations that demand people to think logically. Hence, people are more likely to think logically while making a business decision in a meeting room, than at a carnival while deciding what flavor ice cream to buy.

The Human Mind Is Fundamentally Logical

Like I said before, there are times when we respond to emotional appeals, particularly when we are not very involved in the decision and don't have a lot to lose in case we make a bad decision. There are also times when we respond only to logic, and nothing else.

Have you ever been in an argument with your spouse, parent, or friend, where you are trying to convince them of something that you know to be true, but they are just not having it? In such a situation, logical appeal can prove to be very helpful.

Logic appeals to a person's reasoning ability. So if you want to persuade by using logic, there is only one thing that you need to do: GET YOUR FACTS STRAIGHT!

You can appeal to the logical side of the human mind by presenting hard facts and figures. No, that doesn't mean that you can make facts up and get away with it. You are not Harvey Specter from the TV show Suits. Your facts have to be true.

To achieve that end, you must prepare before you have to present an argument. Look for facts, figures, percentages, and the numbers that never lie, that will support your argument and people are very likely to respond to the logic through facts that you are bringing forth.

One profession that uses logic extensively is law. Lawyers gather proof and evidence to support their logic.

How Logic Effects Every Day Decisions?

When logical appeal is used to make a decision, emotions usually aren't a part of that decision. Here is an example of an everyday logical decision:

You wake up to a bright sunny day. You don't feel like going to work but your wife says: "*If you take today off then you won't be able to go visit your dad on his birthday next week.*"

There you have it. Your wife just appealed to your logical mind and guess what, you went to work. Logical appeal can work in similar ways to persuade people in their daily lives.

How To Use Logic To Influence And Manipulate People?

Use **widely** agreed-upon-knowledge or factual information to build a solid foundation of your argument. Don't just make up stuff.

You can use a fact or event that can be compared to the subject at hand. In this way its logic will be proved. It is called the "if-then" strategy. If fact one is true, then wouldn't fact 2 also be true?

For example: "*If thousands of children starve in Africa every year, **then** wouldn't they benefit from financial aid?*"

When the audience is given a solid comparison, it becomes very hard for them to provide counter arguments because sound logic is hard to argue with.

If you want to persuade people, find out their preference for logic or emotion in that particular situation. Follow their preferences and you will definitely have them persuaded.

Here is how you can actually use logic as a psychological trigger:

1. Use "if-then" sentences: "If fact A is true, wouldn't fact B also be true?"

"If you say that you would like to have a lawnmower that requires minimum maintenance, wouldn't you want it to be of

premium quality with a money-back guarantee?"

See how the if-then logic was used in the above sales blurb for persuasion. Note down five such sentences in a notebook, or on your tablet, and use them within the next week. Logic, like other psychological triggers, requires practice.

Chapter Summary: The Key Points

- The three rhetorical appeals given by Aristotle are Ethos (the credibility of the speaker), Pathos (the emotional appeal), and Logos (the logical appeal).
- There are certain personality types who are mostly inclined towards making decisions based on logic. There are also certain situations in which people are mostly inclined to respond to logic.
- To use logic for persuasion, you need to get your facts straight. One example of a logical appeal is an "if-then" sentence i.e.

if fact A is true then fact B must also be true.

- Do not rely on make believe, lies or off the cuff insight. Know your stuff!

Chapter 5: Feeling Of Significance

"People will forget what you say, but they will never forget how you make them feel."

Everybody, I repeat, everybody in this world likes and wants to feel important. So a very simple way to get people to do what YOU want is to make THEM feel important.

I Am Important

It has become incredibly difficult to achieve success in today's world. A very important ingredient for success is the ability to be influential and persuasive. A great way to be persuasive is to make others feel important.

Let me tell you a little secret about people. People WANT to feel important. So, by making them feel important, you will only be giving them what they already want. There are several ways to do it:

1. **Express your gratitude:** Whenever there is an opportunity, don't forget to

mention that you are grateful for whatever the other person has done, or is doing for you. You don't have to act, just be genuinely grateful for whatever service the other person is providing. When people receive gratitude, they feel like they truly matter. They start to associate these positive emotions with you and there you have it: a recipe for persuasion.

2. **Listen to them talk about themselves:** There are some people who never let an opportunity to talk about themselves pass by. Then there are others who must be given a push to talk about themselves. No matter which category they belong to, almost everyone loves to talk about themselves, what they do and what they love. One great way to persuade people is to get them talking about themselves and to listen to them talk about their life, likes, and dislikes.

3. **Praise them sincerely:** I am not saying that any kind of "butter them up"

approach is key here. Be honest in your praises. When you are, the other person will feel important. Feelings of importance will lead to feelings of happiness and like I mentioned at the very beginning of this book, happy people are easier to persuade and influence.

How Do Feelings of Significance Effect Every Day Decisions?

"Hello there Mr. ... Umm, I am sorry I cannot remember your name, what was it again?"

You just witnessed a persuasion disaster. People feel important when you remember their names, says Carnegie in, "How to Make Friends and Influence People".

Well, remembering names is definitely going to increase your persuasive abilities.

Our everyday decisions are largely based on the notions of importance that we perceive others to be giving us. Imagine that your neighbor walks up to you one morning and says:

"Your parallel parking is just flawless you my friend are a fine driver!"

Well didn't Mr. Neighbor just make your day? This is how sincere gratitude and praise works in persuasion. You are very likely to offer up any favors that this particular neighbor might ask of you later. Babysitting his 2 year old this weekend, are we?

Remember L'Oreal Paris's very popular tagline? *"Because you are worth it!"* You're damn right I am worth it! In fact, I am awesome! That is what every human being on this earth wants to feel. L'Oreal Paris rocketed their sales sky-high by simply using the "I Am Important" psychological trigger.

How To Use Feelings of Significance To Influence And Manipulate People

Like I said before, you can make others feel important in a number of ways: call them by their name, send them a card on their birthday, listen to them actively and respond appropriately, get them to talk about themselves and listen, smile, express gratitude and praise them sincerely.

Influence will work best if, while talking to the other person, you keep their interests in mind rather than yours. You will win hearts if you make use of this strategy.

I am sure that by now you must have worked out a couple of ways in which you can influence people by making them feel important. I want to emphasize again that the goal here is not flattery or trickery, you must be genuinely nice, and if you are too much of a snob to be actually nice, then maybe being influential isn't for you?

Here are some ways in which you can use the "I Am Important" psychological trigger to influence:

1. Tell the person you want to persuade that you like the way they have decorated their office, before starting on the actual matter. Be specific when you express

praise. Don't use something very general, such as, "Your hair looks exceptionally good today." You will get caught out. Use something specific and unique to that person.

2. Use their name again and again during the conversation. This gives a very personal touch to the conversation and it works on a sub-conscious level. If you use a person's name again and again they are going to feel important, without even realizing it.

3. Express genuine gratitude for something they have done. For example, *"I am extremely grateful for all that you are doing by running these schools. It is indeed a great service to our children and the community."* Whatever you say afterwards is going to be high in persuasive appeal, because you have set the right kind of tone building upon it.

Chapter Summary: The Key Points

- Making the other person feel important can be the "royal way to their heart".
- There are a number of ways in which you can make the other person feel important. For example, remembering their names, expressing heartfelt gratitude and praising them, talking about their life, work and interests are all ways to make others feel important.
- When you learn the art of making the other person feel significant, you will enhance your persuasive capabilities a great deal.

Chapter 6: Anticipation

You are going to absolutely love what I am going to tell you in this chapter.

It will blow your mind. Just read on to find out some of the darkest ways to control, manipulate and influence people.

The Psychology of Anticipation

Did you just get very excited about this chapter after reading the above introduction? This, my friend, was anticipation used **like a pro**. I built up enough anticipation before starting this chapter to get you interested, and when you are interested and curious, you are very likely to get influenced.

The psychology of the anticipation trigger is very simple. People love closure. They do not want to have incomplete information and they certainly do not like to be left hanging onto the end of an incomplete sentence. It can really annoy people when you only deliver partial information, leaving some of it unknown, beyond reach and loose. They want, need, even demand the conclusion that you've just built up to but as yet haven't finished.

If they leave after you have just said something that has successfully built anticipation, they have no payoff. The idea that they might acquire more information is an incentive for them to stay.

How Anticipation Effects Every Day Decisions?

I love checking out new food places. Yesterday, I came across a signboard outside "Louie's", with a really adventurous menu listed and a little "Opening soon!" written in the corner of the board. I was excited; I couldn't wait for their launch.

Louie's used anticipation as a psychological trigger in their campaign. Since mentioning this example to you, there must be some several thousand advertisements popping up in your mind that have used anticipation as a psychological trigger. Despite its frequent use, it still works as a great persuasive strategy.

This is how anticipation effects everyday decisions. When you are curious about something and anticipate it, you are very likely to be persuaded. That is why you get very excited after watching teasers and trailers for movies and new TV series. They develop your interest before the Big Show.

A great example of how to use anticipation in product-launches is given by Apple. Have you ever noticed how thousands of people get in line to buy the new Apple product that hasn't even been released? Apple builds anticipation for all their products before releasing them.

Another great example of anticipation as a psychological trigger is The Super Bowl. Weeks before the event, months even, people from all over the United States start to plan and anticipate the day. This is the case with many other sporting events too. The thought of watching a big sporting occasion with friends, while enjoying their favorite foods and drinks, gets people excited several days, if not weeks, before the action even starts.

"Anticipation is a key stage in happiness" – Gretchen Rubin.

The anticipation trigger caters to our desire for pleasure by bringing us something that we can look forward to and be excited about. This way, happiness makes its way into people's life even before the actual event takes place.

Some big brands even have websites that are just for rumors related to their products. The anticipation built as a result of these rumors increases their sales.

How To Use Anticipation To Influence And Manipulate People

1. Whenever you intend to launch a new product or service, if you are in the sales and marketing profession, use anticipation. Don't just launch the product right away and then have your

potential customers decide whether they want it or not. Start with some teasers, that will help you grab their interest and when they are interested, they are half-way persuaded. They are on their way to buying into your product or service.

2. To use anticipation in persuasive writing you must use short and memorable sentences. Read the beginning of this chapter again and look at the sentences. They are simple, short and are a perfect way to boost your curiosity about this chapter.

3. In public speaking, the anticipation trigger can be used to gather people's attention. "Do you want to know a big psychology secret? Do you want to achieve success within the next year?" This kind of questioning fills people with anticipation. Anticipation then leads to persuasion and that means control.

4. Simple phrases like "Wait until I tell you about it", or "Coming Soon" can achieve the buildup of the audience's anticipation.

5. One way to build anticipation is to talk in the future tense, for example: "Once you have bought this Jacuzzi, you will be able to enjoy the weekends with your family and friends." In this way, the listener visualizes him or herself using the product, their anticipation about the product increases when they visualize all the fun they are going to enjoy.

6. Another way to increase anticipation is to have people sign up for your product so that when it is released, they can be given a "heads up". This gets people really excited about the product before its release.

Chapter Summary: The Key Points

*   A great way to persuade is to use phrases that build the reader's or audience's

anticipation. Several advertisements use this technique.

- Anticipation works because human beings have a need for closure or complete information. When they get curious, they want to know more.

- Anticipation can also be used in public speaking and writing to garner the listeners and readers' interest. Once they are interested, they are very likely to be persuaded and thus controlled.

Chapter 7: Relating To Others

In previous chapters we talked about the fundamental human needs we have and how the need to relate to others is one of our most important desires. The necessity to relate is third in the hierarchy of 'needs', and it is an expression of our innate tribal nature. For example, others will like us and will want to befriend us if we are helpful and kind to them.

The Need to Relate

There are many species in this world. Some like to live alone, while others like to live in groups. Human beings are very social and of course belong to the latter category. Living in a group has its perks; the work is divided among many and you are relatively safer --unless, of course you turn on each other in which case you are either ruined or running for your life!

There are some downsides to living in groups. For example, you have to follow the rules of society and its regulations. However, the perks obviously outweigh the downsides and human beings, as a result, are programmed to have a need to belong. Which makes us form groups, communities, and tribes.

Having Common Interests and Enemies

Groups have common interests and enemies. For every person, there are many in-groups (the groups they belong to), and out-groups (the groups they do not belong to). People identify with their in-groups. For example, if you are a US citizen, America is your in-group whereas the rest of the world is an out-group.

Now, would you say that as a US citizen, you have some common interests as all other Americans? Similarly, would you say that you have some common enemies? That is what makes the need to relate such a powerful psychological trigger. Our need to relate gives us many common interests and enemies with our **in-group** and our behavior is guided by the need to relate to that in-group and its resulting community, be it a family sized one, or an entire nation.

How Does the Need to Relate Effect Every Day Decisions?

If you bought a piece of merchandise displaying an American flag on the 4th of July, the seller used your need to relate to make that sale. Your need to look and feel American compelled you to buy a shirt, a hat, or a badge adorned with the American flag.

Nowadays there are many groups that we might want to join. If you just got an expensive club membership then it is because of the fact that you have a need to relate to the club members.

If you are aspiring to get a job at one of the leading advertising agencies of the country, then you have a need to relate to that company, and that is going to drive your job hunt.

How To Use the Need to Relate To Influence And Manipulate People

You can use the need to relate to influence, manipulate, persuade and control people.

1. First of all, find out what groups the other person belongs to, and what group do they aspire to belong to. You can either use the values and needs of that group to suit your purpose, or you can work to weaken their ties to their group so as to get your own way.

2. Sometimes, you can influence people by joining the same group as your mark. For example, if you are targeting a person who is a member of a golf club, you might have to go golfing to persuade them. (Even though you might hate it!)

3. In turn you can also get people to join your group to influence them. Once they attach themselves to the values of your group, it will be easier to persuade them.

4. If you hold a position of power within your group, then it might work in your favor to promise to include or threaten to

expel a certain person who you want to control. The fear of being expelled from a group will make people comply. People often use this approach --usually very subtly so that they do not appear mean, because once you appear mean, you can lose the trust and respect of the groups' members.

Chapter Summary: The Key Points

- The need to relate is one of the needs in Maslow's Hierarchy. We are social beings and we need to form groups, communities, and tribes.
- Our need to relate to our **in-groups** often guides our behavior and decision-making, a trait that can be used against us by compliance professionals.
- To use the need to relate, you might have to join the target person's group. Conversely, you can include him in your group. The latter will work amazingly if

you hold a position of power in your own group.

- You can practice influence on a person by threatening to exclude them from your group. Conversely, you can persuade them by promising privileged inclusion to a certain sought after group, for which you hold the key.

Chapter 8: Authenticity

In the "Logic" chapter, I elaborated on the three modes of persuasion given by Aristotle i.e. Ethos, Pathos and Logos. Ethos, in this trio, refers to the credibility of the speaker and thus, the authenticity of the information that is being provided to us. The speaker, through their character, conveys a lot of information regarding the authenticity of knowledge that is being provided to us.

We Need Proof

Human beings want to make informed decisions. We need to know if the knowledge being provided to us is authentic, and whether the speaker is a credible person. We can say that one source of authenticity of knowledge is the speaker's character. Aristotle's ethos aims to show the speaker's trustworthiness. Thus, the speaker must aim to "appear" trustworthy. It will be great if he IS trustworthy, but Aristotle's ethos merely talks about the appearance of trustworthiness.

How Authenticity Effects Every Day Decisions?

We are more likely to get persuaded when we believe that the information that is being provided to us is authentic, or is coming from an authentic source.

My father asked my husband to choose one product from a number of inflatable collars that were available online. My husband is knowledgeable in the area of online shopping, and my father felt that whatever he chose for him would be a good quality product. Thus, my father believed in the authenticity of knowledge that my husband was going to provide, because his credibility, as a smart online shopper, had already been established in front of my father.

This is how our beliefs about authenticity of knowledge can affect our everyday decisions. There can be people who we believe to be credible, and there can be other sources, for example a particular magazine or website, that we consider to be credible. Information coming from those sources will be more persuasive for us.

I always make my online purchases from Amazon. Why? Because its credibility has been established through experience. The products arrive on time and are of good quality. If I don't like the quality of the product and return it, I know that Amazon will refund my money without question. So, the performance of a source builds its credibility, thus building our beliefs about the authenticity of information coming from that source.

How To Use Authenticity As A Speaker To Influence Or Persuade An Audience

Using the authenticity trigger to influence an audience is simple. You must first build your own credibility as a speaker. There are several ways to do so:

1. Trustworthiness of the speaker is established by his body language, content of speech, vocal characteristics etc. You must research and get your facts straight before speaking to an audience. Provide proof of your statements whenever possible. For example:

"You can read about Maslow's Hierarchy in Hierarchy of Needs: A Theory of Human Motivation by Abraham H. Maslow."

Note that the complete name of the book and author is provided, which tells the audience that the speaker / persuader has researched the subject well.

2. There are other ways to plant authenticity beliefs in the audience. You must portray yourself in such a way that your authority is established. That is, you must **seem** like an authoritative person. Studies show that people are more likely to get influenced by a person who expresses very

clear signs of authority e.g. wearing a suit with a tie. So, if you haven't been paying attention to the way you dress, now is the time that you should start doing so.

3. Work on building your reputation. Always provide quality work or service and make sure you deliver on time and keep your promises. This will quickly build your reputation and your reputation will precede you anywhere you go.

4. A great way to build reputation is to have an established feedback loop through positive word of mouth. There can be many ways to start this positive word of mouth feedback loop. For example, you can ask some people to leave positive reviews on your website or blog.

Chapter Summary: The Key Points

- A great psychological trigger is to make your words sound authentic. There can be many ways to achieve that, one of them is to establish your own credibility as a speaker.

- Other ways to achieve authenticity is to research your facts well. Maintaining quality of work and service also helps in achieving authenticity. Your body language and appearance have a great role in establishing authenticity. So work on your appearance and gestures if you feel that you were neglecting them before.

- Build your reputation by using positive word of mouth, which is also a great way to appear authentic.

- Remember, it is great to be authentic, but it is also super important to APPEAR authentic.

Chapter 9: Curiosity

"This is not just a phone..."

Did you want to read on and know what else "this" is besides being a phone? The above line was successful in arising your curiosity, and so are many other lines in the world of persuasion and influence.

Humans Are a Curious Species by Default

You cannot persuade anyone without first getting them interested in what you have to say, and curiosity is a great way to fuel people's interest. Curiosity can be defined as the desire to attain more information about something. Everyone is overcome by this desire several times during the day and without us knowing, it sometimes even guides our decision-making process.

Curiosity stems from knowledge gaps. We can define a knowledge gap as the difference between what a person has in their knowledge bank and what they would like to have in said knowledge bank. According to Menon and Soman (2002), curiosity arises when a person is aware about the existence of a knowledge gap. Curiosity motivates us because we would like to attain more information to fill the gap in our knowledge.

Curiosity works best when some information is provided, while some is kept from the customers. When most of the information is provided, the curiosity of the customers diminishes. When too little information is provided, it fails to generate any curiosity in the potential customers.

Compliance professionals usually give you an itch that needs to be scratched. In the world of Neuro-Linguistic Programming (NLP) it is called "opening a loop". The person that you intend to persuade must close that loop by listening to what you have to say.

How Curiosity Effects Every Day Decisions?

Many of our everyday decisions are affected by curiosity. Did you just decide to read a certain book till the end? It is because it kept your curiosity levels high. Did you just decide to get tickets to a movie after watching the trailer? It is because it fired your interest.

Did you just stop at an advertisement while flipping through the channels? It is because it triggered your interest. Did you just click on a link from your social media profile homepage? Exactly, curiosity!

Did you just decide to watch a TV show till the end because they gave you snippets of what was coming up next? That was inquisitiveness taking its toll on you.

How To Use Curiosity To Influence And Persuade People

1. Questions: The best way to evoke curiosity in people is to ask questions. If you ask a good enough question, people are going to get motivated to know what you have to

say. For example: *Do you think you can lose 15 pounds in a week?* This kind of question will compel the audience to go on listening to whatever the persuader has to say.

2. Fright Challenges: Fright Challenges are a great way to arouse curiosity, and a little bit of fear among people. You will be amazed to know that generating a little bit of fear in the audience actually compels them to listen to what the persuader has to say. Joel Bauer, in his book "How to Persuade People Who Don't Want to be Persuaded", gives several examples of Fright Challenges.

"What you are about to hear is a bit disturbing, in fact, it would be a smart thing for you to shut this book right now and put it down **immediately**..."

Now, wouldn't you be compelled to put the book down and listen to what I have to say until the end? This is how a fright challenge works. It gets an audience's or an individual's immediate attention. All due to the fact they are curious because of the possibility of an imminent danger or fear. Once they are intently listening they are open to being persuaded or influenced.

3. Cliff Hangers: In books and TV shows, the psychological trigger of curiosity is often used in the form of cliffhangers. How often have you read the next chapter of a novel, or watched yet another episode of a season just because you want to know what happens next? I know I have spent HOURS hung up on a TV show, all because they used cliffhangers. So, if you are aiming to persuade people by using the mediums of writing, cliffhangers are a proven way to do so.

4. You can use curiosity in everyday settings to influence and persuade. For example, if you are trying to get a date with a girl that you like, and she doesn't seem very interested, try this: *"We will have a wonderful time. I cannot tell you exactly where we will be going, but I promise you'll want to go again. "*

5. You can use curiosity triggers in parenting as well. For example, if your kid doesn't want to go to bed at bedtime, you can show him a box and say: *"If you want to find out what is in this box, you will have to go to bed right away and I'll let you have a look inside early in the morning."* Chances are that your child will comply, and if he doesn't, well there are many other techniques in this book that you can use. You will just have to keep on reading to find out.

Chapter Summary: The Key Points

- Curiosity is one of the most powerful psychological triggers. It can be used in writing and speaking to get people to listen to and comply with whatever you say.

- Curiosity works because we want to fill the gaps in our knowledge i.e. the difference between what we already know and what we would like to know. In terms of NLP, curiosity works because compliance professionals "open a loop" that has to be closed by acquiring complete information.

- Curiosity effects our everyday decisions in several ways. Several advertisements, TV shows, and movie trailers make use of the curiosity trigger to keep us interested.

- Curiosity triggers can be used in everyday settings, for example in getting dates and in getting your children to comply with what you say and want from them. You just have to practice and get the hang of using it correctly by actualizing the help given in this book's examples.

Chapter 10: Social Proof

"Hundreds of people choose Sunwing Resorts for their holiday…"

You must have seen countless lines such as these in advertisements. Why is that? Why do you care if hundreds of people choose something? The thing is, you do care. You care more than you think you do.

By saying that hundreds of people choose a certain thing, the advertisers create an image of the products' popularity. We are given proof that several others like us have chosen a certain brand for themselves.

Have you ever found yourself looking around for other people, to see if they are doing the same thing as you are thinking of doing? If they are going where you were thinking of going? Have you ever done something that others are doing, mainly because they are doing it, and for no other reason at all?

In a traffic jam, if the driver of one car makes the decision to turn around, many other cars start to follow. This is due to the fact that human beings often make decisions based on social proof.

Social Animals Require Social Proofs

Human beings require social proof to determine what is right and what isn't. We have a basic tendency to think that if others are doing it, it must be right.

By the way, do you think that what everyone is doing is always right? I am sure you don't. Despite the fact that we understand that the correctness of something isn't proven by the fact that many others are doing it, we are often dragged into doing that exact thing simply because others are doing it.

Every fashion trend gains popularity through this mechanism. Social proof is the reason why some very ridiculous fashion trends emerge and stay for a long time. Sometimes, compliance professionals can create the illusion of popularity when in fact; there was never a demand for the product that is now in everyone's closet.

Okay, why do you think sitcoms have canned laughter? No one really likes it. However, psychologists conducted research in which they found that jokes that were followed by canned laughter were found to be funnier by the audience. Why do you think that is? Exactly, it is due to social proof. Canned laughter produces an illusion of social proof. Everyone knows that the laughter is fake, yet it works on a subconscious level and it's true that we do laugh harder at the jokes followed by canned laughter.

How Do Social Proofs Effect Every Day Decisions?

The first time I went to a Tutti Frutti Frozen Yogurt Bar, I was unfamiliar with the ordering process. So, guess what I did? Instead of asking for instructions, I just looked around and did what the others were doing. That way, I saved myself the trouble of asking for instructions. We do things like this all the time. We look around for social proof while making several buying decisions. We look for social proof before getting persuaded.

So the next time you buy something because it is the "biggest selling" brand of the year, or the "fastest growing" telephone network, take your time and think again!

How To Use Social Proof To Influence, Persuade And Manipulate People

Social proof can be one of the best ways to persuade, manipulate, control and influence people.

1. Consider this, you have just put up a stall showing of your product at a fair and are desperate for some attention and even though you know your product is top-notch no one is really taking interest in your wears. Here is what you can do to fix that:

Pay some people to form a little crowd, and many others will be drawn towards that little crowd, making it bigger. Are you having doubts about this because it sounds too manipulative? Here is another way: Hire a renowned crowd-gatherer who will bring people to your stall. If that isn't possible, start a competition of some sort. Just get SOME people --in any way possible-- and I guarantee, more will follow. Crowds create an impression of popularity and when several others receive this cue for social proof, they just follow.

2. You can use social proof to help people with problems, especially children. Children who have specific phobias, for example, a phobia of dogs or rabbits, can be shown videos of other children playing and touching dogs without any sort of fear. Research by Albert Bandura revealed that after observing other children play with dogs in a video clip, 67% of the children became willing to play with and touch dogs. When a number of children are shown doing the same thing, the

results are improved i.e. when social proof becomes greater, the magnitude of improvement also increases.

3. Social proof can also be used to help children who experience a problem with socializing. Robert O' Conner conducted an experiment in which kids with a social isolation problem were shown video clips of other children who were socially isolated at first but who, later on, engaged in social interaction with other children and ended up being happy. After watching the clips, the children overcame their shyness and became very friendly and social. The children from the control group, who weren't shown the video clips, showed no improvement in their problems with interaction. You can also use social proof by showing others videos of people doing what you want your target person to do, but be subtle about it.

4. Whenever someone seems to be unsure or unclear about something, that is when they are most likely to fall prey to social proof. Similarly, when we see that many others who are similar to us are doing something, we are very likely to become a victim of social proof. If people providing proof are different from us, then it becomes less likely that we will do as they are doing. So, while using social proof as a psychological trigger, make sure the proof you are providing is similar to the target person's. Next time a customer walks in, unsure about what present to buy for a child , tell him that the XYZ toy (the toy you actually want to sell), has been become incredibly popular and that most parents have been opting for this as The Gift to give their children. In fact, you have just restocked after you ran out!

Chapter Summary: The Key Points

- We often look for social proof i.e. whether other people are doing something that we are thinking of doing, before making decisions.

- Social proof is a great psychological trigger and is widely used in advertisements.

- Despite being aware of the fact that social proof is something that compliance professionals use for their purposes, we often fall prey to it because it works on a subconscious level.

- Social proof can be used to help people in trouble. For example, children with phobias can be shown videos in which other children just like them are playing / or handling the object that they fear. Research has shown by doing this it alleviates the symptoms of phobia.

- If you want people to pay attention to a product, create social proof. If that isn't possible, create the illusion of social proof.

Chapter 11: Scarcity

"Registration will be done on a first come, first served basis. Hurry up, there are only a few slots left."

I read this sentence on the website of a drama class arranged by a struggling actor. The psychological trigger of scarcity can be well understood by hooks such as these. You will be tempted to join this class, even though you might not have much time to get involved in such activities at the moment. This is the psychological trigger of scarcity and you can use it for your benefit in a number of situations.

The Psychology of Scarcity

According to Robert B. Cialdini, the author of "Influence: The Psychology of Persuasion", when availability of opportunities is limited, they seem more valuable to us.

We are more open to influence when we feel that we might lose something, than when we feel that we might gain something. The potential loss pushes us into action.

One classic example of Scarcity are the Black Friday Sales. Black Friday only happens once a year, and we will buy all the things that we can, even the things we don't need on this day because it is such a scarce day, that we feel compelled to act. To buy! To spend and get everything we can lay our hands on.

"The rule of the few", or scarcity is an amazing psychological trigger. Human beings are attracted by limited availability. This is probably the reason why the Huayra by Pagani created such madness among filthy rich car-lovers. Only four of these cars were made, demonstrating to us a perfect example of the power of scarcity. The idea of "potential loss" compels us to make a buying decision almost immediately. It is also interesting to know that in human nature, "potential loss" works more powerfully than "potential gain".

I mentioned before that the human mind seeks simplicity. Scarcity triggers also provides our mind with a short-cut. Rare = Valuable, your mind makes this connection quickly.

The fear of losing control and freedom of choice compels us to make a decision immediately. We do not want miss the opportunity to choose, so we react by choosing without wasting time. This phenomenon is called psychological reactance.

Research has proved the principle of scarcity. In 1992, Worchel presented some research participants with cookies. The cookies that were put in front of the participants in smaller quantity were rated as more valuable and tasty. Moreover, when we know that the public demand for something is increasing, and its availability is decreasing as a consequence, we are drawn to it like iron filings are to a magnet!

How Scarcity Effects Every Day Decisions?

Once I was really confused by a decision to buy a pair of Jordans. I liked them, and sort of needed them for the gym membership that I had signed up for, but they were a bit too expensive for my liking. That is when the salesmen said, "Only two pairs are left in stock", and that was it, I took out my credit card and made the payment, and went home with the sneakers a very satisfied customer.

Did you notice that for all I knew, the salesman might have been lying about what the store had in stock? He used the scarcity trigger on me and without even realizing it, I fell prey to it. This is how the scarcity trigger effects many of our decisions every day.

Similarly, I bought a ticket to an art gallery, because it was open to the general public for just one day. I like art, but would I really have gone if it was open all the time? Maybe, but I don't know for sure, and I will never know because I went, because it was ONLY OPEN

FOR ONE DAY. This, right here, was a beautiful scarcity trigger in action.

We often have no or minimum self-interest when scarcity strikes. We sometimes go for things just because they are scarce. They become valuable to us only because they are rare.

How To Use Scarcity To Influence And Manipulate People?

1. To increase demand in target markets, several of the luxury products are made in limited number. "Limited edition", they say, and we are drawn to them like flies to a sticky cake. After every few years, blackberry launches a phone in collaboration with Porsche. It's always a "limited edition" and people start to yearn for it days before its launch. So, if you want to manufacture something that sells like it is going out of the shops faster than it can be made, put a tag of "limited edition" on it.

2. You can use the scarcity psychological trigger in similar ways to influence, manipulate, control, and persuade people. If you have an online store, try writing "only two/three items left in stock", underneath the products, then wait and see the magic.

3. If you want your wife to agree to buy a lounge couch that you absolutely love and she doesn't really approve of, try telling her that it's the new "in thing", and the stores are going to run out of these couches very soon.

In short, the ways in which you can use the scarcity psychological trigger to influence, persuade and manipulate are in no way scarce. It is a very handy tool for influence once you get the hang of using it effectively.

Chapter Summary: The Key Points

- Scarcity, or "the rule of the few" is a psychological trigger in which we are drawn towards the things that are rare.

- It is due to the fact that we perceive rare things as automatically valuable.

- Compliance professionals use scarcity to get their way all the time. It is why "limited time offers" and "limited editions" work.

- You can use scarcity in "persuasion" scenarios other than for sales; for example, you can use it in parenting and relationships.

Conclusion

Everyone wants to be successful. In the ever more competitive world of today success has become a much harder objective to achieve. Understanding the science and art of persuasion, manipulation and influence will assist you in your journey towards success **every step of the way**.

Psychological triggers are important in the world of persuasion: A clear understanding and the knowledge of how to use them can help you get a YES out of practically anyone.

Knowing how to use the pleasure-pain principle, curiosity, authenticity, social proof, scarcity, basic human needs, feelings of significance, logic, anticipation, and the need to relate --as psychological triggers-- will help you gain control over all the interactions you have with people. You will be able to get your way with the added advantage of making others happy while you do so.

So, after reading this book, the next step has to be the implementation of all you have learnt. Use your understanding in your everyday interactions and with everyone you meet. With practice, determination and the careful application of your newfound skills you will become a leader in persuasion, control and influence. All of which will secure you an easier path to your destination: Personal success.